Ian Moore founded and ran t[…] Advanced Management from 1[…] business last year. By the time he [was?] multimillionaire. This was largely due to a piece of paper on which he had written 'I am a multimillionaire'. Ian is a withdrawn personality who now lives in exile in Rio de Janeiro following a killing he made on the Stock Market.

Peter Fincham is an expert in middle management and has managed many middles in his time, including a spell at the Middle Temple and a holiday job as a janitor at Centre Point. Peter's expertise in management largely stems from his time at the London School of Economics, where he picked up a lot of tips. Now that he is no longer working as a doorman, he is able to put his many theories into practice. His name appears on the front page of the *Financial Times* every morning . . . mainly so the paperboy delivers it to the right house.

Rory McGrath knows nothing at all about management. He got involved because he was at school with the other authors and has been a bit down on his luck lately, what with his wife running off with a stuffed giraffe. He then hit the bottle, and got a nasty graze on his knuckles. The doctor gave him six months to live, but gave him another six months when he found out Rory couldn't pay his fees.

Illustrated by Nigel Paige

Also available
Cricket Made Silly
Money Made Silly
Food Made Silly
Sex Made Silly
Skiing Made Silly

Management

MADE SILLY

BUSINESS ACUMEN PILLS

Rory McGrath, Peter Fincham and Ian Moore

CENTURY

LONDON · AUCKLAND · MELBOURNE · JOHANNESBURG

Design/Gwyn Lewis
Graphics/Ian Sandom

First published in 1986 by Century Hutchinson Ltd,
Brookmount House, 62–65 Chandos Place, Covent Garden,
London WC2N 4NW

Century Hutchinson Publishing Group (Australia) Pty Ltd,
PO Box 496, 16–22 Church Street, Hawthorn, Victoria 3122

Century Hutchinson Group (NZ) Ltd,
PO Box 40–086, Glenfield, Auckland 10, New Zealand

Century Hutchinson Group (SA) Pty Ltd,
PO Box 337, Bergvlei, 2012 South Africa

ISBN 0 7126 9581 8

Filmset by Deltatype, Ellesmere Port
Printed in Great Britain in 1986 by
Hazell, Watson & Viney Ltd, Aylesbury, Bucks

Authors' Introduction

It is difficult to overestimate the importance of management in the modern world, and yet most books on the subject do so by suggesting that it is the be-all and end-all of existence. But then the authors of such books probably know be-all about anything else.

Not for them the joys of family life, carefree moments of relaxation over a pint of best bitter, or the casual acceptance of life's ups and downs. But then again not for them the tiresome responsibilities of management either, which they have given up in order to write books.

Well, what is management about anyway? Management is about the business of organization. Or to put it another way, it is about the organization of business. Or to put it another way still, management is about ten letters long.

It has been said the development of good management practices is essential to the establishment of a successful and economically viable corporate organization. In fact this was said by an incredibly boring Canadian in the station buffet at Crewe, but fortunately there was no one else there to hear him.

The Birth of Management

- Management is sometimes regarded as a 20th-century phenomenon, ranking alongside other advances of the modern world such as TV quiz shows, nuclear bombs and Aids.
- But in reality management has existed since the dawn of time (not to be confused with the time of dawn, which is of course when all good managers get up).
- But let us go back to the Stone Age. A grim swamp-ridden period with few pleasures and only the occasional visit by Dr Who to break the monotony.
- In the Stone Age life was cruel, life was hard. Ideal conditions for the thrusting young executive. Early man had decisions to make . . .
- Should he get out of caves and into wattle-and-daub huts?
- Should he sponsor cave paintings or did beaker-manufacture look the better long-term prospect?
- Was another tribe going to come along and wipe out his fortified village? Perhaps he should consult his stockade broker.
- His capacity to take these decisions was hampered by his inexperience of management methods, the daily grind of having to try to corner the market in dinosaur meat ('make a killing' as it came to be known), and by the fact that language had not been invented yet. Or was it? How far does conceptual thought require the

existence of verbal ability? Many a philosopher and linguist has suggested that conceptual thought cannot pre-date the existence of something that can be described as 'language' or 'words' or 'quotation marks'. On the other hand, a New Guinea tribesman whose recently discovered culture possesses no known language has recently said, 'Grrrrrr umpffff dridddle wurps'. So there you have it.

- But I digress. (If that's the word for it.) Until some proper management structure could be devised, all early man could do was to beat people over the head with clubs and keep quiet about his invention of the wheel until somebody else invented the Patent Office.

- Civilization just could not get going until somebody was able to start bossing somebody else around.

- It was probably in Egypt that this was first appreciated. Certainly it is there that the earliest traces of business methods are still to be found — the Pyramids. Later to become famous as the name of a way of selling things to gullible people, the Pyramids are a monument to the techniques of company management — a corporate structure if you like. The Pharoahs correspond to today's shareholders: rich blighters who sit around doing nothing but own everything and want to take it with them when they die. Their soldiers and courtiers correspond to the management of today, organizing the workers, or 'slaves' as they were then called, into doing the actual work. The slave-workers toiling through the desert with the blocks of stone for the pyramids were operating within a primitive but effective incentive scheme: get on with the work or we'll kill you.

- Management had been born.

Getting on with People

Whatever the field, management is almost always about managing people. It is therefore vital that you get on with them. Here are some important things to remember about people . . .

Unless you work in advertising, the majority of people you meet will be human. This fact is a great advantage for the smooth running of a company. As a general rule humans don't wrap themselves around you and try and kill you by constriction, nor do they buzz around the room banging their wings on the light bulb.

Human beings usually talk English (except of course foreigners and Geordies. It is therefore unadvisable to work with these people unless you're a foreigner yourself . . . or a Geordie, a language teacher or a diplomat).

People come in all shapes, sizes and colours. The shape and size of someone should not influence your behaviour towards them, and neither should the colour unless of course it's bright green with big yellow spots. This can mean one of three things: he's seriously ill, a Martian, or an over-zealous Norwich City supporter.

People in offices and big companies can be subdivided into the following categories.

(1) bright and hard-working

(2) bright

(3) hard-working

(4) keen and efficient

(5) stupid and lazy

(6) the people working for you

Here are some useful phrases to encourage the people working for you and to show that you are pleased with their work and wish to reward them:

Well done!

Good work!

We'll have to review your pay at the end of the month!
Get your laughing tackle round this!

Here are a few phrases you may find counterproductive:

'Did you take lessons to become that thick, or is it a gift?'

'A friend of mine is looking for accommodation; I hear the inside of your head is free.'

'I'm afraid the three-day week finished in 1974.'

'Congratulations, I hear you're the only known survivor of a braintransplant . . . and you were the donor.'

'If I said you were the company's greatest worker . . . I would only be two letters out . . .'

'You like playing games during office hours, so here's your cards.'

Although people can be good fun to talk to, drink with and do rude squelchy things with . . . they can be made to feel angry, hurt, depressed and dangerous when you tell them how useless and incompetent they are. And the most bizarre thing about this behaviour is that it has little to do with whether or not what you say is true! So remember . . . if you have to sack somebody, be as fair as you possibly can . . . sack everybody.

Napoleon

Napoleon managed to become Emperor of France despite being a mere Corsican corporal. He is chiefly remembered for saying 'Not tonight Josephine' and by the joke:

Q: Where did Napoleon keep his armies?
A: Up his sleevies.

Apart from winning lots of battles at places which were to become French railway stations (and then losing one at Waterloo), Napoleon was a dynamic manager of the French state, introducing such things as the metric system and wide roads in Paris. Despite his great perception and intelligence, he was fundamentally a jumped up little oik driven by a need for self-aggrandizement. If he were alive today, he would probably be running an oil company.

One interesting fact concerning Napoleon is that many madmen think they are Napoleon, whereas Napoleon thought occasionally that he was mad. Actually that isn't all that interesting, but it's the sort of thing that Michael Caine might tell you.

Meetings

A Typical Chairman's Agenda for a Vital Board Meeting

(1) Go to the lavatory and take lots of tranquilisers. Look at self in mirror. Think how unfit and old I look. Worry about wife finding out about 'that incident' with Hilary two months ago.

(2) Check with Hilary that meeting is still on. Is it too late to cancel?

(3) Pick up any old piece of A4 you see lying around and pretend that's your agenda for the meeting.

(4) Walk briskly past boardroom. Hope that no one's there yet or if they are, hope they don't see you.

(5) Go to the lavatory to check that you look all right. You don't.

(6) Barge into boardroom looking as if you mean business. You don't. The others notice it.

(7) Decide to be firm and to start by saying, 'Let's make this meeting short and to the point, because we all know that meetings are essentially a waste of good working time.' Chicken out to say, 'Morning, gentlemen . . . er . . . hello, Basil, how's Jean?'

(8) Note Basil's reply with special attention to his wife's name: Sheila.

(9) Ask for the minutes of the last meeting to be read out. Make a note of anything important that happened in the last meeting. Nothing . . . except you called Basil's wife 'Susan'.

(10) Sit up shocked and surprised when the minutes have been finished and people are coughing and saying, 'Excuse me, sir, are you all right?'

(11) Start controversy about the minutes in the vain hope of putting off present meeting as long as possible.

(12) Discussion about last minutes are brought abruptly to a halt by that pushy git from Accounts who says, 'Let's get down to the business of this meeting.'

(13) Noting that there is NO business of this meeting, you order up more coffee and biscuits . . . try and remember the tea-lady's name and say she's been with the company for 25 years and probably knows more about the company than anyone. Hope to get a laugh. Hope the tea-lady offers to chair this meeting.

(14) The bulk of the meeting. Everyone reiterates what they've already agreed to on the phone, anyway.

(15) Just when you think it's over and no one has noticed that nothing has happened except they've had fifteen cups of coffee each, that pushy git from Accounts says, 'Any other business?'

(16) Try and say, 'No, I'm sorry . . . far too busy, must dash . . . lunch appointment' but end up saying, 'Everyone all right for coffee while we go through other business?'

(17) Leave meeting three hours later than you wanted in a cold sweat, determined to cancel all meetings for the rest of the day.

(18) Tell Hilary you're off for a round of golf. Hilary says, 'But, sir, you've got four meetings this afternoon, one in half an hour. The helicopter's waiting, sir.'

(19) Say, 'Oh, very good, Hilary . . . I'll get my brief-case.'

(20) Send memo to yourself re suicide.

Decision-making

The secret of decision-making is knowing your own mind, having the confidence of your convictions and standing firmly behind the course of action you adopt . . . or is it?

The modern manager is faced with decisions on a day-to-day basis, and knows that his job may be on the line if the decisions he takes prove to be wrong.

This is where delegation comes in (see *Delegation*). It might be said that the art of management is taking credit where it isn't due, and avoiding flak where it is due.

Decision-making is a high-risk business which is best left to others. This point at least is worth taking a decisive stand on.

17

In any situation, be it personal or professional, some sort of dealings with other human beings is necessary. The presence of another human being usually necessitates a deception of some sort: just plain lying, distortion of the truth, or concealment of the truth. Here are a few euphemistic phrases one might come across around the office.

Some Business and Management Euphemisms

'He's a really great guy though a lot of people don't like him.'

He's a shit. A lot of people don't like him for this reason. You think he's really great because he hasn't quite got round to shitting on you yet . . . probably because he doesn't think you're important or significant enough.

'A lot of people don't understand him.'
This means either he talks Hungarian or gibberish, or a lot of people don't understand why he's such a shit. The speaker thinks he/she understands him because he/she has fallen for a bunch of lies told in confidence to everybody in the office about personal and family problems weighing heavily on his mind and therefore making him act like a shit, which is really most unlike him.

'He's a really charming guy.'
This is tantamount to saying he is a shit, but he's either flattering enough or witty enough for you not to mind that he's stabbing you in the back.

'He's the sort of guy who'd stab you in the back.'
This is usually said about some totally innocent guy that *you* wish to stab in the back by poisoning other people's minds against him.

'He's a really easy-going kind of guy.'
This is usually said of one's superior who:
- (a) unbeknown to you, has just been sacked, so couldn't give a damn
- (b) has just been diagnosed as terminally ill, so doesn't give a damn
- (c) has just been offered a much better job with another company, so doesn't give a damn
- (d) has just decided to sack you, so is being really easy-going with you until he breaks the news

'Great guy to work for.'
You can safely say this about someone you've never had to work for.

'The people who work for him respect him greatly.'
This almost exclusively means he's a real shit to people who work for him, as it's almost impossible to respect someone who's really laidback and good fun to be with.

'Not a woman's kind of woman.'
This is usually said by women of another woman who is much more successful with men than they are.

'He's been with us for twenty-five years now.'
It's too embarrassing to sack him. We'll offer him a better post in our Inverness plant and he might decide to retire early.

At least this is the implication in the private sector . . . In the public sector, the Civil Service or the BBC, the implications are it's too embarrassing to sack him, so we'll invent a non-existent post and promote him to it.

'He's got personal problems.'
This is usually said of people who drink too much. This affects their work and they invent personal problems . . . like 'my wife doesn't understand me' (this is probably because the drink makes him slur his speech too much) or 'being tired and emotional'. This is all part of 'Newsreaders' syndrome'.

'He's an Oxbridge graduate.'

A rather damning insult in the ruthless world of business and high finance. It means that someone has been formally educated and may prove to be creative and original. He may do things in a way that this company doesn't like things to be done. Can't we hire somebody from a polytechnic . . . someone who's keen and will do what we ask him.

The worry about Oxbridge graduates is of course quite unfounded, as anyone will know who has met the sort of mealy-mouthed upper-class idiots that our two great universities churn out year after year.

The Manager and the Little Man

Mr Small had never felt so proud as when he entered Pizza Paradise with his luscious secretary Shirley Handfuls on his arm. Her tight dress barely contained her lubricious figure.

'A table for two,' said Small.

'Certainly, and what about you, sir?' said the waiter.

Herbert Small, as his name suggested, was a complete herbert. He had started at the very bottom of his company and painstakingly worked his way down to being assistant wages clerk. He lacked talent, ambition and aggression, so much so that he had once been approached by Bobby Robson to play in England's midfield in the World Cup. He was so cautious that he'd even look both ways before crossing his legs. Since his wife left him he had been a shadow of his former shadow. So he had good reason to be proud that he had summoned up all his minuscule will and courage to ask Miss Handfuls out for dinner that night.

She arrived at work at nine-thirty on the dot. She got off the dot and chained it up in the dot park. Small saw his office door open and her proud bust edge round the door. Shirley came in ten minutes later. She had accepted his invitation with alacrity, even promising coffee at her flat afterwards. Something stirred in his loins. It was a teaspoon.

Pizza Paradise had been Shirley's choice of venue for their first night out. Small would have prefered a restaurant, but he was too shy to argue with her. Pizza Paradise was decked out in red checked table cloths and red checked cushions, and the waitresses wore checked shirts and checked aprons. In fact, the only thing that wasn't checked was the sell-by date on the pizzas. They looked horrendous . . . some looked like menstruation on toast . . . some like dried scabs recently dropped off an elephant with scabies. Small ordered the former with extra anchovies.

'This is awful,' shrieked Shirley as she looked down at her plate, where it looked as if a shaved-hedgehog had recently been run over by a steam-roller. 'Mr Small, you must get the manager and complain immediately!'

Small panicked. He had never complained about anything before. He couldn't *possibly* have a confrontation. Not even a heated discussion. Not even a discussion that hadn't been heated. He gulped with fear. The manager!? He was the *boss*. Someone in authority. Someone to be feared and respected. A well-spoken, good-looking young man in a sharp suit who would smooth over the situation with slinky charm while still managing to make Small seem a bolshy buffoon and leave him humiliated in a pool of trembling perspiration. Small couldn't face that! But in the other corner there was Shirley. Expecting him to defend her honour; to stick up for her; to be manly and brave; if he didn't face up to the manager, this could be his last chance to get closer to the glistening banquet of Shirley's body. He gritted his teeth and called the waitress over. The die was cast.

'Sorry to bother you,' said Small, 'but someone's cast this die. Look, here on the floor.' Shirley kicked him under the table and growled 'Jerkoff!'

'Oh yes, another thing . . .' Small sounded as angry as he could. 'I demand to see the manager.' As the words left his lips there was an almighty bang. The glass front of the restaurant had been smashed with a brick. An enormous black car with tinted windows squealed to a halt, and from it burst four men wearing black balaclavas and firing random machine gun shots into the ceiling. Tables and chairs went flying. There were screams, faintings and chaos. The scene was abominable. Two of the men stormed up to Small's table. A foreign sounding voice beneath the dark hood said, 'He's here. This is him.' That was the last thing Small remembered.

After that things went deadly silent and deathly dark. Did he see a sack being put over his head? Did he see the flash of a glass phial and feel the stark coldness of a needle? Did he hear Shirley say 'I love you' as the world of sound and colour ebbed grimly and irrevocably away from him? Had it been a dream? Shirley, the dinner, the attack, the miserable school years, the untainted and untouchable sunny days of a childhood in Devon.

'He's coming round,' an unknown voice shouted, and it echoed around Small's blank dream a few times and then began to make some sense. Small woke up. He opened his eyes to see an intelligent face staring at him.

'I hope you're all right.' And then another voice, a girl's. 'Does His Holiness want anything to eat?'

The first voice snapped back, 'It's not His Holiness. We bungled.'

And then a third voice. 'Shame, I wanted to hear him say "Happy Easter" in eighty-two different languages.'

The first man spoke gently to Small. 'We're a deadly band of international terrorists, and we were going to kidnap the Pope and ransom him. But we made a mistake and got you instead.'

'Oh, I'm terribly sorry,' said Small 'Was it my fault?'

'No, it's all right,' said the first voice, whom Small assumed was the leader. 'But there is one small thing,' he went on. 'You've seen us close up. You can identify us. So we can't let you go . . . or at least we can't let you go . . .' There was an ominous pause as the leader measured his sickening words, 'with your eyes functioning.' A second man approached. He was holding a piece of metal which looked like a surgical tool. Small looked at the pitiless polished steel and the horror dawned.

Another bang. Ears temporarily stunned. Through a stinging high-pitched whine his hearing returned. Smoke and tears. People running past him, ignoring him. Words from the news headlines and screams. 'Terrorist bomb factory accident.' Small was paralysed with fear. He decided just to lie still. No. He changed his mind . . . and later his trousers, and ran like hell. Everything had happened so quickly that he felt he was ahead of reality. The reality of running through the dew-sodden green of rural England, a burning house behind him and behind him also the rose pink promise of a night with Shirley. His first thought was to hide. They would be after him. He had seen them and would recognize them again. Four people wearing black balaclavas over their faces wouldn't be difficult to spot in a crowd. In a lane by a field he saw a small van, the back covered by a canopy. As he climbed under the canopy he heard a jet flying overhead. Low. Engines slowing down. Landing. He was close to an airport. In the back of the van there was a large laundry basket. He climbed into it, hunched himself into the corner, and waited for something to happen.

Sleep happened. He was awakened in the basket by something moving. Whatever he was resting his head on was moving. Something long, cold, slimy-green. Something that hissed. 'Oh my God,' thought Small, 'a hissing cucumber.'

Small fainted, and the 30-foot long anaconda slithered irritably around in his basket, under Small's back, through his legs and over his face. The snake listened to the meaningless noises of the airliner hold—the high-pitched engines, the clanking of the undercarriage, the stewardess's footsteps above, and had no idea he was being returned to the wild until he was dumped from a Brazilian forestry-commission helicopter along with Herbert Small into the oily yellow water of the Amazon.

For weeks Small wandered in the jungle, living off berries, fruit and the rotting husks of strange fish discarded by alligators. A group of friendly Guarayina Indians mistook him for their messiah returning from a millenium in the underworld of Ulruluru. They bedecked him in gold and blue jade and he slept with a dozen fourteen-year-old brides. He officiated at the festival of the tree-frog and danced the Cucarrascu completely naked but for a sacred dung beetle tied to his genitals. The tribe was attacked by their war-like neighbours, the Fufuarami, but Small was able to buy his freedom with a large bag of coca leaves. He was given a canoe and for ten days drifted with the current till he arrived at Manaus. In a bar there he asked for the British Consul and was mistaken for a visiting English professor.

For three months he taught at the Institute there, and managed to pick up a smattering of Portuguese, enough to be able to talk his way into getting a posting in London. But an abrupt change in government saw a fiercely xenophobic régime come to power and many foreigners were discredited. Small, while waiting for his plane to London, had two kilos of heroin planted on him, and when the plane was refuelling in Cairo, it was searched and Small's stash was found. The rest of Small's life was now ruthlessly mapped out, with thirty years in a tiny, dank Egyptian jail with no light by which to identify what blind insects were crawling over his naked body and no sound but the scuffling and scratching of fetid rats. But the Fates shook their dice one more time for Herbert Small. Double six. And a careless prison guard gave Small another chance and he snatched at it.

Disguised as the hump on a camel, he made it to the harbour and slipped unnoticed onto a Greek merchant ship. But he was tired of running and hiding. Greece was a Common Market country. He could safely give himself up. The last six months had made him a new man, confident, brave and dauntless. Using his few phrases of Portuguese and lots of extravagant hand gestures he managed to tell the Greek captain his story, and on their arrival in Athens he was met by a government limousine and taken to the British embassy. He was ushered into a large room, completely empty but for the pompous portraits of potentates past and present.

Small had been alone for nearly an hour before the door opened and a man wearing a red checked shirt and badge saying 'Manager' walked in.

'I believe you wanted to see me, sir.'

Small gulped with fear.

'About this pizza!' he eventually stammered.

'What about it?' challenged the manager.

'Oh, nothing.'

Delegation

One of the secrets of management is delegation, which in plain language means getting someone else to do the work for you.

It could even be argued that delegation *is* management, or vice versa, since the whole point of being a manager is that you do the managing while the workers get on with the working.

Delegation is particularly prevalent in hierarchies, and the greater the hierarchical structure, the more delegation is likely to go on. Thus the chairman delegates to the general manager, who delegates to the head of department, who delegates to the supervisor, who delegates to the shop-floor workers, who just delegate.

In this way nothing gets done, but each person has someone else to blame, so everyone is happy.

Motivation

Motivation is a rather vague and ill-defined concept which usually merits a section in books about management, so why should *Management Made Silly* be any different?

Because we can't be bothered, that's why.

THE CONTENTS OF THE EXECUTIVE BRIEF CASE

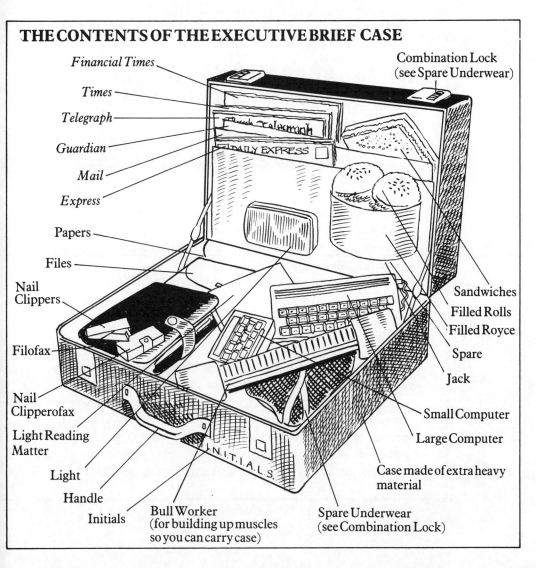

- *Financial Times*
- *Times*
- *Telegraph*
- *Guardian*
- *Mail*
- *Express*
- Papers
- Files
- Nail Clippers
- Filofax
- Nail Clipperofax
- Light Reading Matter
- Light
- Handle
- Initials
- Bull Worker (for building up muscles so you can carry case)
- Combination Lock (see Spare Underwear)
- Sandwiches
- Filled Rolls
- Filled Royce
- Spare
- Jack
- Small Computer
- Large Computer
- Case made of extra heavy material
- Spare Underwear (see Combination Lock)

27

One-Minute Management

According to a best-selling book on the subject, all decisions in business life can be taken after no more than one minute's thought. At least I think that's what it said; I only spent 60 seconds reading it.

But is it necessary to make up your mind so quickly? Most top managers would say yes, as it means there is more time left over for getting to the golf course, having lunch, playing with your executive toys etc.

The important thing is to be dynamic. See the problem, think it through, make your mind up, write a memo, change your mind, tear it up, phone your wife, dictate a letter, flirt with your secretary, change your mind again, take away the number you first thought of, make a final decision, work out a way of blaming someone else if it all goes wrong. And if you can do all that in a minute, you can look forward to promotion or a heart attack in eighteen months' time.

★ Vending Machines ★

Introduced to most big city offices to encourage people not to waste time leaving the building and walking down the street to Luigi's Sandwich Bar. Modern vending machines offer a wide variety of hot and cold drinks and sometimes supply a paper cup with the drink. This quite often comes a little bit too late. A typical selection of vending machine drinks would be as follows:

light brown water (dangerously hot)

dark brown water (dangerously hot with five sugars)

frozen still orange (warm)

fizzy orange (still)

still orange (but only just)

boiling red liquid (slight soup flavour)

Like all slot machines, the vending machines are heavily prone to jamming . . . you can get round this problem by nipping down to Luigi's for one of his excellent large espressos.

Books about Management

The modern manager's life is a hard one, packed with decisions, meetings, research, golf and the sheer 24-hour grind which being a manager entails (though some work a slightly shorter week — 23 hours). So one thing the modern manager definitely hasn't time for is indulging in something as non-productive and self-indulgent as reading books.

Which makes it all the more strange that bookshops are full to bursting with books on the subject of management.

These fall into the several distinct categories:

(1) I Made It!

Cliché-ridden rags-to-riches tale written by some American megalomaniac who has spent thirty years building up his business from a small workshop above a shop to the multi-million-dollar corporation we all know today, and who decides that it's time to write a book explaining to the rest of the world exactly how he did it and how we could do it too if only we were as unbelievably brilliant as he is. In the meantime his business goes bust.

(2) Management is Like Playing in the Nursery

Patronizing drivel written by some so-called Professor of Management Studies who thinks that if he reduces all he knows about management to the level of Enid Blyton, budding young managers will read it and suddenly be transformed by its elixir-like powers into budding Richard Bransons.

(3) In Search of a Quick Buck

Pseudo-scientific nonsense written by a couple of sycophants who have spent the past couple of years fawning over the supposedly great managers of today in the hope of learning the secret of good management and possibly in the hope of getting a job, and who think that if you write a book long and tedious enough on the subject, management will end up seeming like a science.

One thing links all these books about management: they aren't worth the paper they're written on. Furthermore, although they sell in vast numbers, it seems reasonable to assume that few people ever bother to read them from cover to cover.

And yet they make their authors a great deal of money!

Which shows that the authors of these books have at least stumbled on one golden rule of business: if you can sell people something they don't really want and pocket the money before they've cottoned on to the fact that they don't want it, who gives a damn anyway?

Sexual Harassment

One of the most complex problems of modern life. Nobody, psychiatrist, feminist, boss or secretary, nobody is quite sure whether it's *HAR*assment or ha*RASS*ment. One thing is certain: sexual harassment usually, though not exclusively, concerns women. Just think in how many ways they harass men. They have bosoms. Things that crave attention simply by sticking out of the chest in that typically bosom-like way. And as if that isn't bad enough in itself, the bosoms have on the end those little nipple-like devices known as nipples which, especially in breezy warm weather, are tantalizingly visible. Then of course there are girls' bottoms. These are almost always attached to girls. And how they stick out, especially when the girl bends down to pick up that paperclip you seem to keep dropping on the floor.

And in addition to all that, there are legs, ankles, calf muscles, hair, eyes, lips and those little high-heeled ankle booties. Is it any wonder that men are constantly harassed in the office?

Management Types

The 'little Hitler'

In any large organization you will always find a 'little Hitler' — a short fellow who dresses in jackboots, wears a black moustache and goes around whistling 'Tomorrow belongs to me'.

Best either to ignore him completely or remind him about Stalingrad.

The 'slimy git'

Plenty of these in most organizations. This sort of manager will claim to be putting in a good word on your behalf to the boss while surreptitiously trying to have you transferred to another department.

The 'old bore'

Almost any manager who has been with the firm for about thirty years, can't understand why he's been invited on to the board, and is convinced that the only problem with the company is that it is run by complete fools (excluding him), qualifies for this description.

The 'jolly type'

Almost as annoying as the old bore. Most offices seem to have their fair share of jolly types, who are the management equivalent of those tea-ladies with laughs like an express train approaching a tunnel.

The 'pushy twat'

Some young oaf in his late twenties who never leaves the office before seven o'clock. Watch out for this one, because unlike the others, who probably think you've got your eye on their jobs, the pushy twat has probably got his eye on your job.

The 'dull person'

Every office has one well-meaning, inoffensive, conscientious and incredibly dull person whose birthday gets forgotten by everyone else year after year and who you feel reasonably guilty about finding a pain in the neck.

The 'perfectly charming, enormously talented chap liked by everyone and destined for the top'.

You

Hierarchies

What exactly is a hierarchy?

A hierarchy is a structure by which managers at a certain level within an organization are responsible to managers a bit further up, who are responsible to managers a bit further up still, who are responsible to managers so far up that they are responsible only to the board of directors, who in turn are responsible to the shareholders, who are responsible to no one.

In this way it is ensured that nobody is ultimately responsible for anything.

Hierarchies are in some respects unsatisfactory, but are generally thought to be preferable to 'cooperatives' or 'workers' collectives', where the management abdicates responsibility and the whole thing degenerates into directionless anarchy (see British Leyland before Michael Edwardes, Fleet Street before Rupert Murdoch, the England Test Match team under David Gower etc.).

The diagram opposite shows the structure of a typical hierarchy. If you find it confusing, turn it upside down — which is what the people on the bottom floor would simply love to do.

HIERARCHY

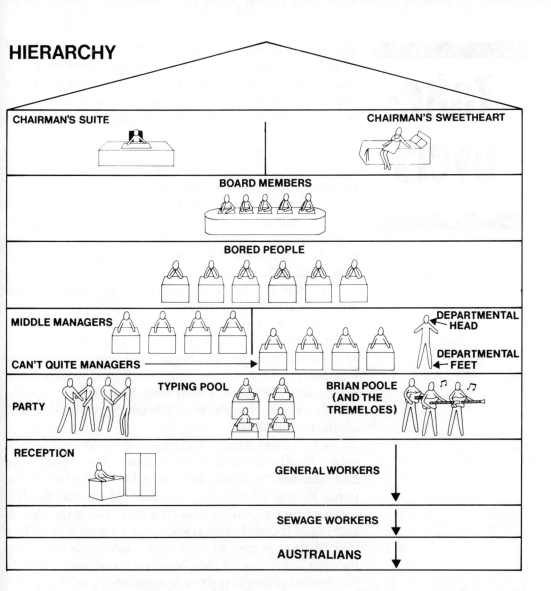

Take-overs

The basic principle of a take-over is very simple. The board of directors of one company offers another company a great deal of money on the basis that the board of directors of the other company step aside and the new board of directors takes over. Thus inheriting all the intractable problems that the first board of directors had to struggle with.

You might think, under these circumstances, that money would change hands in the opposite direction, but big business works in a mysterious way.

What then happens is that the board of directors that has done the taking over indulges in a spot of blood-letting or asset-stripping, depriving all the old directors of their Rolls-Royces, 'rationalizing' the business and giving a lot of people the sack.

They then buy Rolls-Royces for themselves on the basis that the other lot had them, so why shouldn't they?

Then things settle down for a while.

Until another company decides it's time for a take-over and the whole process gets repeated all over again, with the previously new but now old board of directors being ritualistically deprived of their Rolls-Royces.

Nobody really benefits from this merry-go-round, except of course Rolls-Royce.

One of the odd aspects of take-overs is that the vast sums of money bandied about are largely illusory. Thus when United Ball-Bearings Plc whacks in a £260 million offer for international Bicycle Chains Inc., it's quite likely that the first company hasn't got more than a million or two in the bank. It gets round this with what is known as a 'rights issue' which basically means that, in return for acquiring International Bicycle Chains, United Ball-Bearings themselves give away a piece of the action in their own company.

Perhaps this agreeable way of proceeding should be extended to other areas of life. You could, for instance, offer only a small proportion of the cover price of this book — say 20p — on the basis that we, the authors, could have a number of pages from some other book in your collection.

It's an interesting idea, dependent on what other books you have in your collection.

You haven't got any decent porn mags, have you?

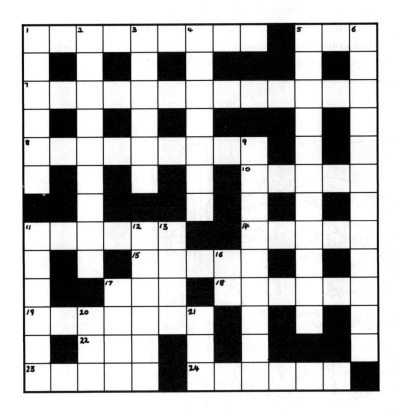

40

Management Made Silly

Across

1/ Conference group gives work to others. (9)

5/ One joins physician to form computer company. (1,1,1)

7/ Efficiency study confuses North in an intimate mood. (4,3,6).

8/ Try to write a longer word. (9)

10/ Exalt English dead. (5)

11/ Advanced king bird is chest-like. (6)

14/ Flower is one involved in traditional teaching. (5)

15/ Board game gives aspiration to the soul. (5)

17/ Short message — on Mayday? (1,1,1)

18/ Southern hairstyle can cause worry. (6)

19/ Kill the executive that has lost four. (7)

22/ See something enormous in go-go dancer. (3)

23/ Bad characteristic of climber. (5)

24/ Transforms King with five points. (6)

Down

1/ Jobs suited for relocation. (6)

2/ Cripple avoids people in debt. (4–5)

3/ Initially German historian and zoologist after lunch, spells out Persian verse form. (6)

4/ Edward, in short, promises to be boring. (7)

5/ First steps from sin I vitiate. (11)

6/ Women in charge, as Regan seems in a muddle. (12)

9/ Key in relation to economic measure. (9)

11/ Property-like groups. (6)

12/ An endless idea, nevertheless. (6)

13/ Cardinal festival without hesitation. (4)

16/ Feminist manuscript. (2)

17/ Way round company tax. (4)

20/ First person in Rome. (3)

21/ Vincent's cut-off point. (3)

*Answers on p. 96.

Crossword

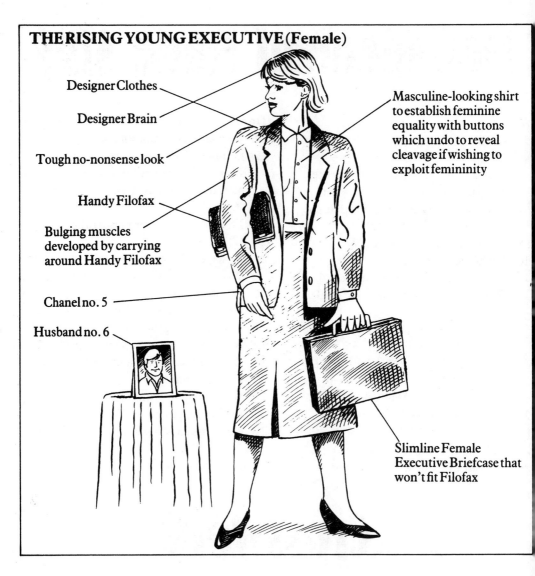

THE RISING YOUNG EXECUTIVE (Female)

Designer Clothes

Designer Brain

Tough no-nonsense look

Handy Filofax

Bulging muscles
developed by carrying
around Handy Filofax

Chanel no. 5

Husband no. 6

Masculine-looking shirt
to establish feminine
equality with buttons
which undo to reveal
cleavage if wishing to
exploit femininity

Slimline Female
Executive Briefcase that
won't fit Filofax

Thinking

Strange as it may seem, one of the most important aspects of a manager's job is thinking.

Not that this is something you can afford to be seen doing in public. When the head of department pokes his head round the door of your office, you want to be discovered doing, not thinking.

Thinking somehow doesn't seem to count.

But the successful manager manages to find a little time each day to concentrate on the broader, strategic vision of management. This may be at the most unlikely times, such as while travelling on the train, or soaking in the bath.

It's not surprising that Archimedes was lying in the bath when the theory of whatever it was came to him and he leapt out shouting 'Eureka!'

Otherwise he'd have been answering the phone, or approving invoices, or filling in the VAT returns.

We all of us need to stop doing things every now and then, and think completely uninterrupted for a few minutes. I'm going to do so right now.

Ah, that's better.

How to Dress at the Office

Anyone who knows anything about business will tell you that it's important to dress properly in order to succeed.

The watchword is *image*. Or possibly the keyword is image. To be safe, make sure both your watch and your keys look right.

Whilst you should never judge a book by its cover (not if you're on the Booker panel at any rate), remember people often judge you by your appearance. So clothes are obviously pretty important.

If you're seeking to create a responsible, sober, sensible sort of impression, you really can't beat a pin-stripe suit. The expression 'pin-stripe' is a rather odd one, because as you may have noticed, pins very rarely have stripes. But three-piece suits do, and they are the standard 'professional' or 'City' uniform. If you are a beginner, be careful not to confuse a three-piece *suit* with a three-piece *suite*, as there is nothing more ridiculous than an office junior arriving in a sofa and two armchairs.

If on the other hand you wish to create a slightly more up-to-date, more go-ahead image, you could startle everyone by coming to work in a two-piece suit with no stripes.

On no account ever be seen in less formal clothes whilst at work, unless you are in a field such as advertising where less regimented clothes are allowable, indeed compulsory.

THE RISING YOUNG EXECUTIVE (Male)

Buttoned Collar

Buttoned Lip

Lean Hungry Look

Thinning Hair

Thickening Wallet

Top Pocket

Bottom Pocket

Bottom

Nerves of Steel

Balls of String

Executive Briefcase

Executive Sandwiches

Sober Suit

Pissed Shoes

Shine you can see your face in (also on back of trousers)

How to Become a Manager

Becoming a manager isn't something that young children dream of.

Pop star, international footballer, astronaut, engine-driver — these are the sort of professions that most eight-year-olds set their sights on.

It's not clear why this is the case. Most eight-year-olds come from families well-stocked with accountants, filing clerks and marketing managers. So why can't they dream more realistically about becoming assistant manager in the local branch of a regional building society? Perhaps this is what the children of sportsmen and entertainers do.

Nevertheless it is a fact that a large proportion of eight-year-olds, whatever the nature of their childish aspirations, grow up to become managers of one sort or other.

There are two possible reasons for this:

(**1**) In the world we live in, there's simply an awful lot of managing to do.

(**2**) Sadly, there isn't that great a demand for pop stars, international footballers and astronauts. (Or engine-drivers for that matter — see *Choosing Your Industry: Nationalized Industries*.)

So let's start from the assumption that, though it pains you to admit it, you're going to end up as one of that distinctly unglamorous breed: a manager.

How do you set about it?

The first thing is to work quite hard at school, and do quite well. Note the use of the word 'quite'. It certainly won't do to work *too* hard: this will be bad training for your future working life. And by the same token, it won't do to do *too* well, or you may inadvertently end up as a professor of nuclear physics.

Statistics show that most managers are in the B stream at school. The chaps in the A stream are altogether too bright and are destined for university degrees and exalted careers in the Civil Service or the professions. Don't worry yourself unduly about this: they'll end up making far less money than you.

And the chaps in the C and D streams aren't cut out for management: they're cut out to be workers, or maybe cut out altogether and will join the other four million on the dole.

So assuming you've done moderately well at school and kept out of trouble, you will probably find yourself at seventeen with absolutely no idea of what you want to do with the rest of your life. This makes you ideal management material.

The next stage is to keep an eye on the 'Situations Vacant' column in your local paper.

And the next stage after that is actually to reply to some of the advertisements.

Henry Ford

Henry Ford undoubtedly qualifies as one of the great managers of history, which would annoy him if he were still alive today, since he took the view that all history is bunk.

Come to think of it, he thought that all managers were bunk as well. And that all beds were bunk.

But he did invent the idea of mass production, and his company made millions of Model T Fords, which he himself wished to call Model T Bunks. He is famous for saying you can have it any colour you like as long as it's black, hence his nickname 'Lenny Henry Ford'.

Alf Ramsey

Alf Ramsey was famous for winning the World Cup in 1966, and was an expert in delegation — such as getting the England team to play the football while he himself sat on the bench. The first modern manager of the England team, Alf managed to persuade the footballing authorities that if he was going to make a success of it, he, and only he, should select the team.

The footballing authorities accepted this, and after England failed to get beyond the quarter finals in Mexico in 1970, returned the compliment by demonstrating that they, and only they, were entitled to give Alf the sack.

He has never been heard of since.

Management Made Silly Quiz

(1) Is your expenses claim . . . ?
    (a) a work of art
    (b) a work of fiction
    (c) the only work you ever do

(2) 'If America sneezes, Europe catches a cold.' Explain this doctrine in connection with the AIDS epidemic.

(3) Is a capitalist . . . ?
    (a) someone who lives in London
    (b) someone who buys shares in London
    (c) someone with more money than a socialist

(4) If asked if delegation was the mark of a great businessman, would you . . . ?
    (a) agree
    (b) disagree
    (c) get someone else to answer the question

(5) If asked to work on a Saturday, would you go to the office in . . . ?
    (a) casual dress
    (b) formal dress
    (c) trousers

(6) **Would you describe yourself as . . . ?**
    (a) a self-made man
    (b) a selfish man
    (c) a self-made woman
    (d) a shell-fish

(7) **Who would you describe as the best at managing in the world today . . . ?**
    (a) the Americans
    (b) the Germans
    (c) Terry Venables

(8) **Spot the odd man out . . . ?**
    (a) General Motors
    (b) General Electric
    (c) General Accident
    (d) General Robert E. Lee

(9) **If you were to put yourself in the shoes of the Chairman of ICI, would you . . . ?**
    (a) continue to invest in the UK
    (b) expand your overseas portfolio
    (c) hope he hadn't got verrucas

(10) **Is 'bottom-up management' . . . ?**
    (a) a form of plastic surgery
    (b) one of those meaningless terms people use in the titles of their books on management, business and related subjects

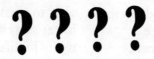

The Perks of Management

Gone are the days when the badge of office in the average industrial concern was the key to the executive lavatory. Well, they never really caught on as badges. Not very beautiful to have your chest decorated with a Yale key with 'WC' written on it in Snopake.

In these more egalitarian times everybody has to use the same washrooms and eat in the same canteen. But there are a range of newer perks for the management. Number one being the business lunches you can have on expenses which, apart from anything else, keep you away from the works canteen.

Number two is the company car. There's something quite weird about the importance that is attached to the company car. Apart from salesmen, nobody needs to have a car for their work. But the chairman must have a chaffeur-driven limousine for his personal use and everybody in upper middle and lower management must be provided with his Sierra or Rover or BMW or whatever. It is supposed to have something to do with tax, it being just a shade harder for the Inland Revenue to get hold of 30 per cent of a car than it is to dock your pay.

From the company's point of view, company cars are good news because their employees are kept in a perpetual state of paranoia about their status, comparing the size and performance of their vehicles with each other, like small boys inspecting each other's conkers. Other status symbols are the standard of carpet in the executive's office: its size, quality and shag pile.

And there are the secretaries (selected on much the same grounds).

Most executives don't need a secretary. They could perfectly well do with the occasional use of the typing pool and training in how to use a desk diary. But without a secretary the executive would have to tell his own lies when he did not want to speak to somebody, and would have to stay married to his first wife for the rest of his life.

Exclusive Interview

By the shrewd use and timing of his superb management skills, Maurice Conningham-Shyster has become one of the richest and most influential businessmen of international finance. Usually shy of the limelight, he gives few interviews with the press, so we were delighted and honoured when he granted our team of *Management Made Silly* reporters this EXCLUSIVE INTERVIEW.

Maurice Conningham-Shyster is a tough man. And when I say 'tough' I really mean 'Scottish', because I was never any good at adjectives. I met him in his office, high above the City of London. His plush leatherlined suite smelt of success. Or possibly a Turkish whore who had just left the room. It was difficult to tell.

Conningham-Shyster sat squarely behind his marble-topped desk. He played with his marble for a while, then commenced the interview. Behind him the oak-panelled wall was bare but for his portrait and a hefty looking safe.

Interview

MMS	Tell us a bit about your background.
SHYSTER	It's an oak-panelled wall with a portrait and a safe.
MMS	All right then . . . let's go back to the very very beginning. How did it all start?
SHYSTER	I think there was a big bang and gases combined to form the first DNA molecule and things slowly grew from those initial building blocks.
MMS	I mean *you* . . . you and your childhood.
SHYSTER	There was a big bang. My mum and dad at it again. I was the youngest of six. We were a very poor family. Sometimes the whole family went without food and water for as much as six weeks.
MMS	That's incredible . . . Most people would have starved to death. How did you cope?
SHYSTER	We didn't; we starved to death. But I had a Scottish mother and a Jewish father, and they managed to get us all to come back to life to avoid death duties.
MMS	Where were you brought up?
SHYSTER	In the roughest, toughest parts of Glasgow.
MMS	Gorbals?
SHYSTER	No, it's true.
	At this point the interview was interrupted by an important international phone call. His secretary came on the intercom.
SEC	Mr Conningham-Shyster . . . I've got Helsinki on the line. What shall I say?

SHYSTER	Say, 'You're a wonderful city and you really deserve to be a capital, even if it is only Finland . . . I'll take you out for lunch one day . . . when I can find a restaurant big enough.' Sorry, gentlemen. Next question?
MMS	You have a reputation for pushing people around . . . especially those worse off.
SHYSTER	Yes, I admit it. I did in my early days. I pushed people around.
MMS	People worse off than yourself?
SHYSTER	Yes, I had to. I was a hospital porter.
MMS	You are managing director of quite a few successful companies: Making Money International, Associated Robbers/Greedy Bastards Incorporated, and Usingotherpeoplessavingstomakemyownfortune PLC, to name just a few . . . What do you owe your success to?
SHYSTER	Well . . . my great-grandfather said something on his deathbed I'll never forget.
MMS	What was that?
SHYSTER	Aaaarrrggghhh!!!
MMS	Do you have any particular philosophy about being a successful businessman?
SHYSTER	MY motto is this: 'Always trample on people on your way up, just in case you end up staying at the top and don't get a chance to trample on them on the way down.'
MMS	As possibly the busiest man in the world, you

Interview

	must have a pretty full day. What would be a typical day for you?
SHYSTER	I'm up at 6.30 every morning. I put on my tracksuit and running shoes.
MMS	How far do you run?
SHYSTER	I'm far too busy to waste time running. I immediately take my tracksuit and running shoes off and put my city clothes on. It is absolutely vital that I'm constantly informed of every detail of the latest international financial news. I've got to know everything there is to know about it. So I always read that pink newspaper . . . I can't remember what it's called . . . ET or something . . . that's full of numbers and prices and things. I also read one or two of the popular tabloids.
MMS	This keeps you in touch with grass roots culture?
SHYSTER	No, it's the tits I go for. Just a little test to see if I can still muster a hard-on.
MMS	What about leisure? Do you have any time to relax?
SHYSTER	If ever I've got a few days off . . . you'll find me on the golf-course at the crack of dawn.
MMS	You love golf?
SHYSTER	No, I despise it. That's why I go down to the courses so early. I take my pick and shovel and go and hack up the greens and fill in the holes with concrete.
MMS	Are there any sports you like?

SHYSTER	Hang on, I haven't finished slagging off golf yet. Stupid bloody game for smug middle-class wankers in comedy trousers. Ruining good walking country with their poxy flags and red V-necked jerseys. Should have their bollocks removed by law . . . or better still, by blunt carving knives. And as for women golfers, they're even worse. No bollocks to chop off. I think that's all. Next question?
MMS	I was going to ask if there were any other sports you like?
SHYSTER	Can't stand football. Never ever seen an entertaining game of football.
MMS	You're an Arsenal supporter?
SHYSTER	On the contrary, I'm the Arsenal chairman.
	Another interruption from secretary.
SEC	I've got Berlin on the line, Mr Conningham-Shyster.
SHYSTER	I'll take it. Hello? Hello, Irving, how are you? How's the song coming along? Good. I can't talk long, I've got the 'Made Silly' people here. 'Made Silly'. You've never heard of it? Yes, that's the one. Sorry, gentlemen.
MMS	Finally . . . Have you any advice for people who want to become successful in business or management?
SHYSTER	Yes. Never answer stupid questions.
MMS	Isn't that slightly rude?
SHYSTER	Yes. But not as rude as this: 'Piss off, you nosey dickheads. I've got money to make!'

WIN
The Management
RAT RACE

A GAME FOR EVERYONE
FROM 16 – 65 (WHEN
YOU ARE PENSIONED OFF)

RULES

1 **Each player takes it in turn to throw a die to determine how many squares to move his counter along the path of the rat race, apart from the real bastards who grab the die and hang on to it the whole time.**

2 **If you land on a coloured square, follow the instructions, unless you are a real bastard, in which case only follow them if they suit you.**

3 **The winner gets to the piece of cheese first.**

4 **That is always a real bastard.**

4 You win a scholarship to Harvard Bu
School. Miss 3 turns while you are there.
that all your throws count double

5 You read *One Minute Management*. Ther
always take 60 seconds to move your cou

7 At a conference you have an affair with
boss's wife. Have an extra go (with her), th
back 4 squares when your boss finds out

10 You think of an idea for improving effic
which everybody likes. Go forward 2 squ

12 You think of an idea for improving effic
which everybody hates. Go back 3 squar

15 Be sick over chairman at office party. M
turn

16 Chairman is sick over you at office party. M
turns

17 Miss office party. Be sick for 3 turns

21 Your company adopts a youth policy. Ad
1 square for every year you are younger tha
go back 1 square for every year over 30

24 Expose the player due to go next as *ei
pederast with AIDS *or* someone who d
understand computers. You advance 1 s
and the other player misses a turn

27 Read a book which explains how you ca
real success just by reading the book. Adva
squares

30 You are made redundant. Go back to squ

31 You have a heart attack from overwork. M
goes

32 You are killed by a wire-haired fox te
Drop out of the rat race

WIN THE MANAGEMENT RAT RACE

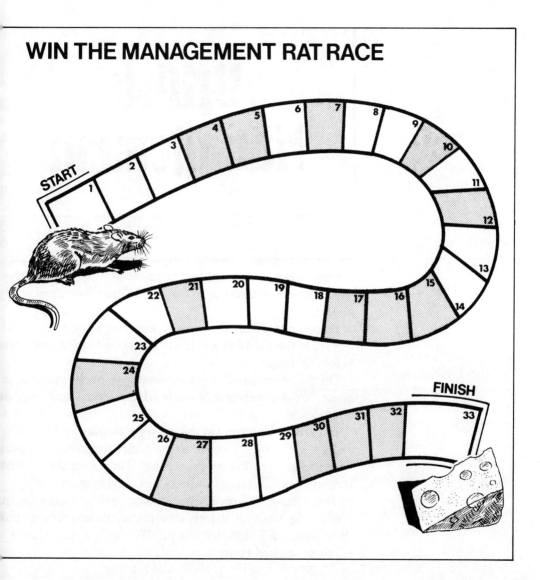

British Management

American managers operate in a fiercely competitive free enterprise environment. Once taken on by a corporation, they work flat out from the age of about 24 until they drop or are sacked.

By contrast, *German* managers work every day, starting at ? o'clock in the morning and rarely expecting to get home again before midnight.

On the other hand, *Japanese* managers prefer never to go home, happily spending 24 hours a day every day at their place of work.

But *British* managers in the main get to work at 10.30 a.m and get home by 5.15 p.m. unless their afternoon golf match happens to take longer than usual. Unaccountably British industry has fared comparatively badly over recent years.

There have, however, been some notable successes in revitalizing flagging British enterprises, demonstrating that there is some life in the old lion yet. Who are the men who have led these spirited efforts?

Eddie Shah

Single-handed Eddie Shah revitalized Fleet Street with his free news sheets in the North of England and the daily paper *Today*. One of Britain's tough new managers. Originally from Persia.

Michael Edwardes

Single-handed Michael Edwardes rescued British Leyland from the brink of losing even more money than it did after he joined. New strong British approach to dealing with the unions. Comes from South Africa.

Rupert Murdoch

Single-handed Rupert Murdoch has revitalized Fleet Street by leaving it and taking his newspapers with him. He is hated by the print unions for being as big a shit as they have been for two hundred years, but shows what can be done in Britain with a stiff upper lip and traditional bulldog spirit. Australian.

Robert Maxwell

Single-handed the publisher of the *Mirror* and rapidly becoming its only reader, Robert Maxwell is one of British industry's success stories, i.e. he has sacked loads of workers. Also scored all of Oxford United's goals. A British institution (imported from Czechoslovakia).

Tiny Rowlands

Once the 'unacceptable face of capitalism', Tiny Rowland's firm Lonrho has emerged as one of the really successful unacceptable faces of British capitalism. Tiny's entrepreneurial spirit demonstrates all that's best in the British spirit of free enterprise. Oddly enough though he's not all that British. Hails from Eastern Europe.

Sir Ian McGregor

Dynamic saviour of British Steel, British Coal etc, Sir Ian McGregor is mainly famous for putting his head in a plastic bag and beating Arthur Scargill to a pulp during the miners' strike. Of Scots origin, Sir Ian is British in every respect except being American.

Freddie Laker

A truly British businessman, Sir Freddie Laker founded Laker Airways and ran it successfully right up until the day it went bust.

Filofax

Filofax are all the rage.

(Or at least they are at the time of writing. By the time you read this, they may be about as fashionable as skateboards.)

What on earth did we all do in the days before everyone had their lives organized by Filofax?

Well, we shall never know, because we didn't have Filofax in those days, so we've got no proper record of what we got up to.

The attraction of Filofax is hard to define. In a sense they are status symbols — the thrusting young executive wears his Filofax like a badge. (Actually this is rather inadvisable, since it can play havoc with the suit you're wearing.)

Nobody could claim that Filofax (or is it Filofaxes?) are practicable. It's all right for women — you just put them in your handbag. But for men it's virtually impossible to decide what to do with them. You can fit your whole life into your Filofax, but annoyingly you can't fit your Filofax into your pocket.

So people leave their Filofax on trains and in restaurants, pick up somebody else's by mistake and find they've got a whole different set of friends and have to go to dinner the next evening with someone they've never met.

Perhaps one day somebody will produce a more convenient version of a Filofax which just lists your forthcoming engagements and a few vital phone numbers, and doesn't include everything from metric conversion to a road map of Sheffield.

This will be called a pocket diary, and will rapidly become the trendy thing to have.

Filofax

William Randolph Hearst

Hearst is best remembered for looking like Orson Welles. So when Orson Welles was directing *Citizen Kane*, based on Hearst, and was looking around for someone to play the title role, who better than Orson Welles himself? A perfect choice, since he was a huge egomaniac whom no one would argue with.

Hearst, the millionaire newspaper magnate, is also well-known for standing in the doorway in *The Third Man* and saying something about cuckoo clocks.

He built himself an enormous mansion in California which he stuffed full of priceless works of art which he begged, borrowed and stole from all over the world. He was widely criticized, mainly by people who thought the treasures should be in the British Museum, which is renowned for housing works that have been begged, borrowed and stolen.

Some Famous Quotes about

'Remember: nobody likes a fawning, sycophantic, flattering yes-man . . . except me. Come and work for me then, my name is P. R. McGrath, c/o Century Hutchinson Pblrs. Ta!'

'Actually, I'd prefer a yes-*woman* if there's one going . . .'

'Good management is about delegation . . . getting someone to do something for you while you get on with something more urgent or important.'

'If at first you don't succeed try, try again . . . and then if you don't succeed . . . sod it! There's no use being a damn fool about these things.'

'The game is not about winning . . . it's about not taking part so you can slag off both the teams taking part.'

'Make a decision . . . right or wrong . . . and stick to it. The important thing is being firm and aggressive . . . if that's all right with you, sir.'

'Oi . . . you! Dickhead . . . come here and write some quotes for me. Here's 20p.'

Management & Success

Types of Manager

The One-Minute Manager

Has read the famous book and hence does everything in 60 seconds or less. Unpopular as a sexual partner and not someone to get to boil you an egg.

The Two-Minute Manager

Like the one-minute manager only twice as slow. Possibly a one-minute manager who stutters. Still not much cop in bed.

The Three-Minute Manager

Unbelievably this fellow wastes a whole 180 seconds thinking about important things before making a decision.

The Four-Minute Manager

A real sluggard, but can just about get through the day as long as there aren't more than fifteen decisions an hour to be made and nobody sends a nuclear bomb over.

The Four-Minute Miler

The most famous four-minute miler of all time is Sir Roger Bannister, who was such a bad business manager he had to content himself with being a world-famous athlete and neurologist instead.

Rules For Executive Success No 23

Negotiation

Negotiation is the process by which two parties — generally the buyer and seller of goods or services — arrive at a price which is mutually agreeable. It is a subtle and elusive art, and has been compared to seduction. In fact the two approaches are rather similar . . .

Negotiation	Seduction
Initial approach to interested party	Initial approach to interested party (often at party)
Take client out to lunch	Take partner out to dinner
Clinch deal	Clinch

Negotiation is something which comes naturally to few people, but which we hopefully get better at with age. Here the comparison with sex ends.

Choosing Your Industry

The eager young school-leaver embarking on a career in management may have ambitions of one day becoming an international tycoon, but first he must make a fairly fundamental decision: which industry to work in.

Getting a job with a firm that supplies cannon balls to the Navy may on the face of it seem like a good wheeze. You certainly won't have to work too hard. But it has to be said that, from a long-term point of view, the cannon-ball industry has been shrinking for some time. In fact it's thinking of cutting its losses and becoming the ball-bearing industry.

The City

This is certainly where the smart young whizz kids of today are to be found. For some time now, all the talk has been of the Big Bang when deregulation takes place, salaries double overnight and everyone gets a Golden Hello. Well, all I can say is I wish they'd deregulate the comedy-book writing business. Advances for writing books are more along the lines of a Bronze Hello, with a Wooden Goodbye to follow if they don't sell enough copies.

Computer and Hi-fi

All forms of hi-tech industry are expanding and worth a look at, though there's always a chance you'll find yourself under a Japanese boss — a hazard secretaries in Tokyo have faced for years. The computer industry has its fair share of celebrated managers, e.g. Sir Clive Sinclair, who falls in the tradition of great English eccentrics — extremely brilliant, endlessly inventive but with a weakness for hairbrained schemes.

Nuclear Power

Working in the nuclear industry is rather like being a member of the government's press office: you spend most of your time worrying about leaks. It is invariably said by opponents of the nuclear industry that it suffers from bad management, which must be galling to managers of the nuclear industry who aren't able to answer back, being extremely stupid. School-leavers contemplating a career in the nuclear industry can take comfort from the fact that it's going to be around for many years to come, or at least the waste is. Like the City, there's talk of there being a Big Bang in this industry one day.

Nationalized Industries

Coal, steel and shipbuilding are the three dinosaurs of modern-day Britain, and very odd names for dinosaurs they are to. Becoming a manager with one of these ailing industries will only appeal to those of a ghoulish disposition. Alternatively, why not join British Rail on a management level? At least you get the chance to go to the famous British Rail charm school, where porters and ticket-collectors are taught how to tell customers that their train has been cancelled/delayed/abandoned/never started out because the driver's a lazy bastard and got drunk last night — all without causing offence.

Fleet Street

For many years now, managers of Fleet Street newspapers have been simply unable to manage. However, now that the major papers are all moving to dockland sites where there isn't a pub for miles around, there's hope of improvement.

On Budget Day the Chancellor, after raising this and reducing that and generally trying to keep everyone as unhappy as they were before, invariably announces a 'package of measures designed to help the small businessman'.

Who is this small businessman, and why does he claim such a disproportionate amount of the Chancellor's time?

And come to that, why on earth didn't all the previous packages of measures do the trick?

Nobody knows.

Nobody even knows who the small businessman is. He is clearly a figure of mythology, like King Arthur or the Lady of Shallott; the difference being that these two aren't thought likely to benefit from an adjustment in the rate of VAT.

Still, if you are a small businessman, it's reassuring to know that everyone seems to be on your side. As Napoleon said, 'England is a nation of shopkeepers'. (This was because he launched his invasion on a Wednesday afternoon and found that everywhere was shut.)

The Small Businessman

Management

Any management which suspects that it is not very good at managing can always these days call in a firm of management consultants.

Management consultants can bring objectivity, perception, scientific analysis and a host of other rather abstract concepts sufficient to charge a whacking fee for, pointing out why things are going wrong, or are likely to go wrong, or have already gone wrong but you just have not noticed yet.

Some questions no management consultant can answer, the most notable being: 'If you know so much about managing a company, why aren't you running one of your own instead of poking your nose into other people's business?'

Consultants

Christmas

Christmas in the office starts at the end of November in order that every department has time to give a lunchtime party.

The sort of things that happen at office Christmas parties have become clichés. Here are some of the common but unlikely myths: all the girls get drunk and take their clothes off; there is a great deal of unbridled sex; people get drunk and tell the boss exactly what they think of him.

The truth is that very little happens at office parties that is different from any other party. People huddle together with people they know, get maudlin drunk and throw up in the filing cabinets (under 'V' if they're meticulous).

Crises

Even the best-organized manager cannot forsee a crisis. What he can do though is plan his day so that some time can be allotted to the unexpected.

Supposing your secretary has to go home ill when it is vital that she is with you in the office. What do you do?

Keep calm, pull your trousers up and get on with your work.

Supposing you're in the middle of a vital conference and the fire alarm goes. What do you do?

Finish your conference, then go and get a new fire alarm.

There's only one thing to remember where crises are concerned . . . the old motto, 'Be prepared'. That old adage was used by Scouts who always had to be prepared, usually be having a thick book down their trousers or making sure they slept further away from the poovey old Scout-master.

Temp

This is short for 'temperamental', and is usually applied to a girl who is qualified as a secretary but is too bad-tempered and moody to keep her job very long.

* Women in *

Increasingly these days jobs which used to be a male preserve are being done by women. And on the other hand, men are sometimes to be found in female preserves (or jams). Management is no exception. It has even been suggested that the term management be replaced by a new word like 'womanagement' or 'personagement' — but only by feminists knowing sod all about the etymological derivation of words.

In all male-dominated spheres woman claim to have to be ten times better than their male colleagues to succeed and point to Mrs Thatcher and say, 'Look over there, it's the Prime Minister!'

Women in management usually suffer from the dual disadvantages of not being able to have affairs with their secretaries and sometimes having to leave to have babies. Other than that, they can compete on equal terms with men, and no one these days would dream of discriminating against them, the dear little things!

* Management *

Deadlines

In most work contexts jobs have to be done by a certain time. This 'time' is known as the deadline. The word is derived from phrases such as 'I wish I was dead' or 'I wish my boss were dead', uttered by people whose 'deadline' is fast approaching.

This expression comes originally from the world of daily newspapers, wherein because of the fast and continual turnover of editions if the news is not written, the paper has to be printed either blank or without news (see the *Sun*, the *Star* the *Mirror*, etc).

There are some important things to remember about deadlines.

(1) They are made up by people who want to give themselves some extra time for looking at the work, changing it, assessing it, etc. So if your boss says he wants some work by Friday the 2nd, it probably means nothing will happen to it for at least a week – the time it takes to get round to looking at it rather hurriedly on the train home or while he's waiting in a restaurant for a colleague to arrive. Therefore for 'deadline' read 'deadline plus seven days'.

(2) Friday: this almost certainly means Monday.

'I must have it by Friday evening at the latest,' means 'I'm going to take it home and look at it over the weekend', which actually means, 'I'm deluding myself that I might actually do some work over the weekend, even though I know I won't feel like it and my wife has organized a hundred and one things we have to do anyway. A hundred and one things I will be able to get out of doing by pretending I have your work to look over, which I won't, even if I *have* your work, which I won't because I know that whenever I say "Friday evening at the latest", you always assume I mean Monday morning, which suits me fine because it means I don't have to do anything over the weekend except watch the cricket and meet up with Basil from the aeromodelling club and have a few jars down at the Bull.'

Middle Management

In the new, lean, cost-cutting environment of British industry, it's usually middle management who are due for a shake-up. This is because top management, while being generally in favour of shake-ups, slimming-down operations and all the other euphemisms for giving people the sack, generally prefer to hang onto their own jobs, and the workers on the shop floor are liable to down tools at the hint of redundancy notices, which is most aggravating . . . particularly in a tool factory.

So it's middle management who get it in the ear.

Middle management is a rotten thing to be in. The very term suggests people who never quite made it into the First XI at school and live in Orpington.

If you find yourself stuck in middle management when you reach forty, while go-ahead types in their late twenties are being promoted above you, one possibility is to look around for a new career.

Another possibility is to do everyone a favour and commit suicide out of office hours.

Doing Without Management

As any radical socialist will tell you, your boss needs you, you don't need your boss. Small comfort when you're self-employed, but no less valid for all that.

The best examples of enterprises without management are workers' cooperatives, of which there are some flourishing examples.

For instance, the Meriden motorcycle cooperative took to making Triumph motor-cycles after Norton-Villiers-Triumph found that they could not make a go of manufacturing them with a traditional management structure. In no time at all the workers' cooperative found they could do just as well as the previous capitalist owners, and went bust as well.

Another example of an enterprise without a manager is the England cricket team. Does it do any worse than the England football team, which has got a manager . . . ? Yes, but then the exception sometimes proves the rule.

Management Titles

If you run a small business employing yourself and a secretary, it doesn't really matter what you call yourself, but in a large organization titles abound, and not all of them describe the job they correspond to accurately — and I speak as executive editor-in-chief of the *Made Silly* series, i.e. the person who checks the manuscript for spelling mistakes.

Life president   The title they finally persuade the old boy to accept when they wanted to shunt him upstairs. Any title including the word 'life' is only bestowed on someone who's likely to be dead within a year or two.

Chairman   The man who thinks he wields the power in any organization but whose only real function is to read out the agenda at board meetings and have a casting vote on issues which are so contentious that whichever way he goes, the company will have fallen apart within a month anyway.

Managing director   The man who *knows* he wields the power in any organization because he gets the blame when anything goes wrong. And also the sack.

Director   Could mean almost anything. Directors of companies include relatives of the chairman, MPs, figureheads and assorted freeloaders.

Non-executive director   A director who has been specifically warned not to interfere with the running of the company. Often the alcoholic younger son of the founder (see *Life president*).

Financial director   Grey-suited, unloved character who was only brought in when the founder and his family had taken the company to the verge of bankruptcy. Makes himself unpopular at board meetings by pointing out that companies with a turnover of £1 million don't usually run three Rolls-Royces.

Public relations officer   The person with the unenviable task of explaining the above titles to outsiders.

Receiver   The person who really wields the power when the financial director's warnings are ignored and the firm goes bust.

Rules For Executive Success No 45

Leadership

Unlike many other aspects of management, I don't think anyone would disagree that leadership is a quality you're either born with or not.

The regional manager of a double-glazing firm can learn all he needs to know about marketing, financial planning and credit control, but it would be hard to teach him the secret of leadership.

Napoleon was a born leader.

Though it has to be said that he didn't know much about double glazing.

Which just goes to show that it takes all sorts and there's nought so queer as folk.

Stress

Stress is something that a lot of people seem to get worked up about these days — in fact there are even books dealing with the tension that can arise from worrying about stress, and vice versa, and coincidentally I'm writing a book on the subject myself, and the manuscript's due in next Tuesday. I've also got *Management Made Silly* to do, and what with my wife being away and getting the kids off to school in the morning, and the problem with the dog . . .

I digress.

The fact of the matter is, we all suffer from stress. The modern manager leads a high-pressure, fast-moving, deadline-chasing life packed with decisions and crises and the constant need to succeed and keep one step ahead of the field.

At least that's his story.

Others may take the view that stress is one of those silly vogue subjects that get written about in the colour supplements and exist largely in the imagination.

I don't suppose our grandparents thought about stress from one year to the next, and what happened to them?

Well, as a matter of fact, they're dead.

The Seven Ages

Of
Management

0	Born with silver spoon in mouth, which is annoying because commodities have been doing badly recently
0·1	Throw up all over mother when silver spoon is exchanged for unit trust certificate
1–3	Infant manager-in-the-making, distinguished by well-fed appearance and pin-stripe romper suit
4–10	'Whining schoolboy creeping like a snail/unwillingly to Harvard Business School'
19	Achieve once-and-for-all sexual peak
20	Kiss girl for first time. . . shame about peaking too early
21	Sleep with girl for first time; peak too early again
22	Start reading the F.T.
23	Still reading the F.T.
24	Finally get to end of F.T. – God it's dull
25	Start to acquire material trappings of success
25½	Give material trappings back when shop assistant points out that you haven't paid for them
28	Young, 'thrusting' stage; chairman reckons you'll go far
29	Chairman is right: he sends you off to manage Saudi Arabian regional office when you're caught thrusting with his daughter
34	Optimum age for manager
37	Optimum I.Q. for manager
38	Impotence creeps in
38½	Wife creeps out

39	Onset of 'God-I'm-about-to-be-40' paranoia
40	Onset of 'God-I'm-about-to-be-41' paranoia
42	Mid-life crisis (wrongly named due to fatal coronary si months later)
45	Spend your time worrying about how to pay the school fee
46	Realise you should have left school twenty years ago
50	Ways to leave your lover
60	Beginning of second childhood (for tax purposes)
64	Absolute pinnacle of power and success
65	Retirement, followed swiftly by senility and death

The Photocopier

A hi-tec machine designed to crumple up sheets of paper. It is an unwritten rule of the office that 'the one nearest doesn't work, but they've got one on the eleventh floor outside the personnel department which works but isn't as good'.

The photocopier is widely used for producing photographic representation of people's bums, faces and hands.

It is a very versatile machine: not only can you photocopy things on it . . . but you can sit on it, place cups of coffee on it, or even walk past it.

Successful Management of Your Time

'Procrastination is the thief of time . . . so try to use shorter words like delaying, putting off, postponing etc.'

When faced with a difficult or unpleasant task it is often quite tempting to put it off until a later date, or better still put it off until a past date and get out of doing it altogether. One of the great procrastinators of history, or at least in Shakespeare, was Macbeth, who put off everything until . . . 'Tomorrow and tomorrow and tomorrow . . .' And it worked for him, because later that day he was killed.

But why is it that when time management is such a key to efficiency and success, so many people are so bad at getting on with their work?

The answer is that they lack motivation. Motivation means having a realistic goal in your mind. And it must be a REALISTIC goal . . . not like the one Pat Jennings scored from his own penalty area that time against Manchester United.

So why not put an end to procrastination immediately?

Stop reading this book and do something useful NOW! I said *now*, you lazy old fart. Look, you're still reading. PUT THIS BOOK DOWN AND DO SOMETHING USEFUL! Look, it's you that'll suffer. Come on, you've got jobs to do, letters to write, phone calls to make . . . Just put the bloody book down, will you? Right that's it . . . I'm coming round now . . . I'm coming round and I'll stuff this book right up your arse if you don't get on with those niggly little jobs! I mean it. I'm ringing for a cab as I type. Right. I'll be there in twenty minutes.

Shorthand

A term from poker meaning a hand dealt from a short pack. In order to make the hands higher, the cards from 2 to 6 are usually removed.

It is also applied to a form of notation based on random and meaningless squiggles which secretaries use for fast dictation and doctors use to write out prescriptions. It was invented by a Jewish coal-miner called Pitman.

Becoming a Better Manager

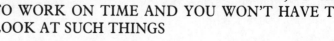

The art of becoming a better manager can be reduced to a few pithy sayings which can in turn be expanded into about a million books on the subject.

Take, for example, 'Don't work harder, work smarter'. This brilliant advice has assisted countless would-be managers, who until they read it in a book thought the way to success was to be found by working their guts out in as stupid a way as possible. *Management Made Silly's* contribution to the store of wisdom-packed phrases on the subject are the following aphorisms which speak for themselves:

TAKE DECISIONS QUICKER RATHER THAN SLOWER
Get it right, not wrong

DON'T BE DUMB, BE SMART
From the bottom the only way is up, unless you are taking off your underpants

DON'T PUT OFF UNTIL TOMORROW WHAT YOU SAID YOU WOULD DO LAST WEEK
The right decision taken now is better than a wrong decision taken later

DON'T RUSH YOUR FENCES
Think positive

USE ADJECTIVES RATHER THAN ADVERBS
The road to Hell is paved with good intentions — any chance of us getting that contract?

THE EARLY BIRD CATCHES THE WORM, SO GET TO WORK ON TIME AND YOU WON'T HAVE TO LOOK AT SUCH THINGS

Glossary

Assembly line (1) Place of dull repetitive work.
(2) Gathering of cocaine addicts.

British Leyland Prestige British company famous for having at one time gone bust. See also Rolls-Royce, Foden, Ferranti, Burmah Oil, and any list of famous prestige British companies.

Carrot & stick An unpleasant way of encouraging people to work harder by offering them a weird salad mixture.

Computer Machine you can count on.

Commuter Man you can count on being held up by the train every other day.

Co-op Store run on non-capitalist lines i.e. not as well as Marks & Spencer.

Coop A place where chickens are kept in close confinement, hence the expression 'batterred up'.

Efficiency A word pointlessly imported into English to describe the way German and Japanese companies operate.

Health & Efficiency Magazine with rather odd photographs of naked people playing with beach balls, looked at by workers and managers when they should be working efficiently (or looking at proper pornography).

IT Originally 'Information Technology', hence any other topic you think you've heard enough about to last you a lifetime.

ET Hideous wrinkled creature who was very famous a few years ago; Michael Parkinson.

DT Always in plural 'DTs', unpleasant mental state brought on by drinking too much to try to forget IT, ET, Michael Parkinson etc.

OTT Dreadful TV programme starring Chris Tarrant (or was it Talent . . . ? No, I think we were right the first time) which was taken off a few years ago because it was one of the few things in life worse than having DTs.

Management buyout Fashionable procedure by which a failing company is sold to its own management, i.e. the very people responsible for its failure.

Middle management One of those 'middle' things that nobody ever has a kind word to say about. Others include the Middle Class, Middlesex, Middle Age, and the Arsenal midfield.

PA Abbreviation for 'secretary'.

PR Public Relations or *per rectum* (i.e what people in public relations speak through).

PE Tiresome lesson at school when you had to jump over things, climb ropes etc. Valuable training for career in management, much of which is spent playing golf, squash, office cricket etc.

PTO Turn page.

Profit sharing Scheme popular with employees until firm makes a loss.

Reverse takeover (1) Procedure when smaller company takes over a larger one. (2) Dangerous manoeuvre on motorway.

Underling Something you put beneath a ling.

Ling Sound of telephone in China.

Unions Organizations to protect the rights of workers, call strikes and so on, much appreciated by high flying managers, as in such expressions as, 'We operate a non-union plant', 'The unions did serve a purpose in their day', and 'Let's sack all the shop stewards'.

Answers

Across: 1/Delegates 5/IBM 7/Time and motion 8/Endeavour 10/Elate 11/Arkite 14/Loire 15/Halma 17/SOS 18/Stress 19/Execute 22/Gog 23/Sloth 24/Renews

Down: 1/Duties 2/Lame ducks 3/Ghazal 4/Tedious 5/Initiatives 6/Manageresses 9/Reflation 11/Assets 12/Though 13/East 16/MS 17/Scot 20/Ego 21/Ear